P9-BII-880

A Word About
Ballet

By Lynne Gibbs   Illustrated by Shelagh McNicholas

ISBN 0-7696-3384-6

50395

9 780769 633848

School Specialty.
Publishing

First published in Great Britain in 2005 by Brimax
Publishing Ltd, Appledram Barns, Chichester PO20 7EQ
Copyright © 2005 Brimax Publishing Ltd
This edition published in 2005 by Brighter Child®, an
imprint of School Specialty Publishing, a member of the
School Specialty Family. Printed in China.

Columbus, Ohio

Library of Congress Cataloging-in-Publication
Data is on file with the publisher.

Send all inquiries to:
School Specialty Publishing
8720 Orion Place
Columbus, OH 43240-2111

ISBN 0-7696-3384-6

1 2 3 4 5 6 7 8 9 10 BRI 10 09 08 07 06 05

What Is Ballet?

Ballet is an art form that combines dance, music, and scenery to tell a story. These young dancers are in a ballet studio where they are learning the basic movements needed to perform a dance. Dancers wear certain kinds of clothing for practice and wear their hair away from their faces.

Clothing

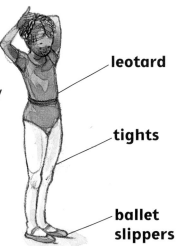

For class and practice, girls usually wear leotards, pink or white tights, and ballet slippers.

leotard

tights

ballet slippers

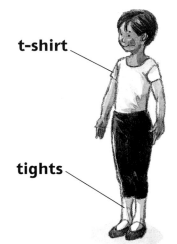

t-shirt

tights

Boys wear leotards or t-shirts, tights, and black or white ballet slippers.

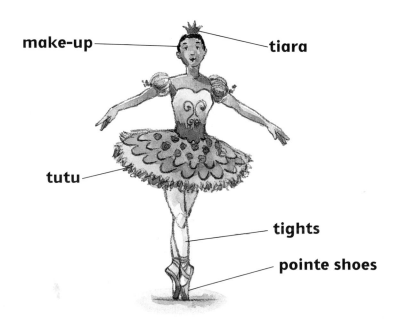

make-up

tiara

tutu

tights

pointe shoes

When ballet is performed, costumes, makeup, and mime play a very important part in the ballet story.

For performances, ballet dancers wear costumes. The style of their clothing and makeup depends on the part they are playing.

Hair

A ballerina should wear her hair pulled away from her face to look neat and to show her features.

headband

bun

braids

Short hair can be pulled away from the face with a headband.

Long hair can be pinned into a bun with bobby pins.

Long hair can also be braided, held back with ribbons, or pinned across on the top of her head.

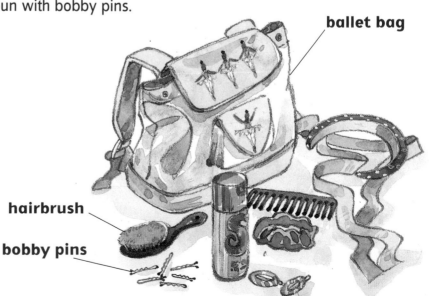
ballet bag

hairbrush

bobby pins

Ballet dancers carry their practice clothing, shoes, and other things that they might need for class in a ballet bag.

Warming Up

Before practice, ballet dancers must warm up by doing leg lifts and other ballet movements at the ballet *barre*.

At the *Barre*

The *barre* is a wooden rail about waist high. The *barre* is attached to the wall in a dance studio. It is used to give the dancer support while exercising. Ballet dancers warm up their muscles by exercising at the *barre* before dancing.

pliés

The first exercise is always the *plié*. *Pliés* stretch and strengthen the legs.

battement tendue

In *battement tendues*, the foot slides out along the ground until the toes form a point. This strengthens the legs and feet.

battement frappés

In *battement frappés*, the ball of the dancer's foot strikes the ground sharply.

The French language

Ballet steps were first developed in France. That is why all ballet movements have French names.

grande battements

Grande battements strengthen the legs and help a dancer raise the legs without strain.

A dancer must have good posture. The head and back must be straight and the hips placed directly over the front of the feet.

Ballet Class

Ballet dancers learn a series of complicated positions and movements in ballet class. They must learn these movements by themselves and together as a class before they can perform in front of an audience.

Ballet Positions

There are five basic positions in ballet. These positions are a part of each step and movement of a finished ballet performance.

Basic Movements

Here are five basic postions for the arms, legs, and feet.

third position
(*en troisième*)

first position
(*en première*)

second position
(*en seconde*)

center practice

Dancers practice their positions during center practice, without support of the *barre*.

fourth position
(*en quatrième*)

fifth position
(*en cinquième*)

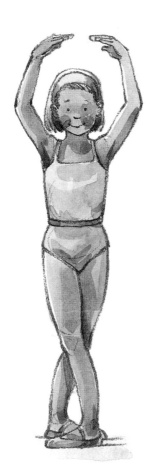

ports de bras

The way a dancer carries their arms is called *ports de bras*. The arms should curve gracefully and the fingers should be slightly curved away from the body.

pointing the toes

A dancer points the toes from the ankle with the leg turned out, called a *turn-out*. The foot should make a straight line with the leg.

Steps and Dances

Ballerinas and ballet dancers have to learn and perform many complicated movements in ballet.

corps de ballet

Dancers often join a ballet company to become part of a *corps de ballet*, or chorus.

pirouette

For this difficult step, the dancer needs perfect balance and strength to spin on one leg.

You can start training to become a professional ballet dancer at the age of twelve. Formal training takes at least two years, working and dancing for several hours a day.

arabesque

This is one of the most basic poses in ballet. The dancer stands on one leg and stretches the other leg out behind.

pas de deux

This graceful, yet difficult, movement requires the male dancer to lift and support his partner.

auditions

Trained dancers have to audition to work in a dance company. This means they have to dance with a group as well as perform a solo in front of experts.

Ballet Shoes

Once a dancer joins a company, she has her own supply of pointe shoes. A dancer wears out about ten pairs of shoes each month!

Ballet shoes are made of leather, canvas, or satin.

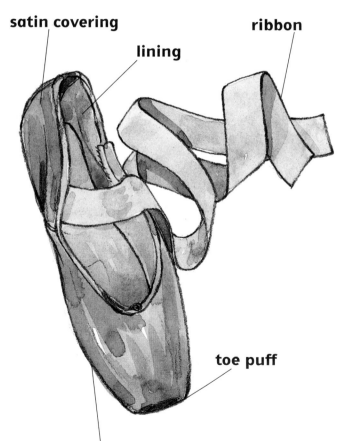

satin covering

lining

ribbon

toe puff

leather sole

En pointe

En pointe is when a ballerina stands on the tips of her toes. To do this, a dancer must be strong enough to lift her body weight to the tips of her toes without straining.

Dancers should not go on pointe before the age of 11. That is because, before then, the bones in their toes are too soft.

The toe of a pointe shoe is hardened with layers of satin, paper, and coarse material called *burlap*.

Shoe Ribbons

Shoe ribbons hold the ballet shoe in place on the foot. This is how they are tied.

Beginners start by wearing ballet slippers held on to the foot with elastic or ribbons. They don't use toe shoes (*chaussons de pointes*) until their bones are strong enough.

1. Start with the inside ribbon and take it over the foot and around the ankle to the back.

3. Both ribbons cross behind the heel and are then brought back around to the front and crossed again, just below the first crossing.

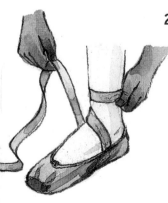

2. Cross the other ribbon over the first one. Then, take it around the ankle.

4. Then, take the ribbons back behind the heel and make a double knot. The ribbon ends should be tucked in neatly under the ribbons.

Young dancers perform their movements together and in sequence so they can dance in front of an audience. While the audience cheers for the ballerinas and ballet dancers, there are other people in the performance whom the audience never sees.

A Polished Performance!

Many people are involved in creating a successful ballet. Technical crew, stage hands, wardrobe assistants, special-effects technicians, designers, and many others are involved in producing a show.

choreographer

A choreographer decides which steps and movements the dancers will make. Then, he or she puts them all together for a finished performance.

stage manager

The stage manager makes sure that all the scenery and props are in place.

lights

Lights help create the atmosphere on stage. Transparent slides of different colors are used to change the shades and tones of a white lamp.

props

Props look like the "real thing" but are usually much lighter. They are used by the performers on stage.

publicity

Posters and advertisements are often printed to tell the public about a show. Programs are distributed at the show that tell about the story and who is performing the roles.

scenery

To make a production look realistic, artists paint lifelike scenes onto a backdrop. There are usually several different scenes used in a performance.

Glossary

arabesque A dancer balances on one leg with the other stretched and raised behind.

audition A try-out that a dancer must make to become part of a dance company.

barre A wooden, wall-mounted rail in a dance studio, used by dancers to balance as they perform exercises.

battement frappés A movement where the ball of the dancer's foot strikes the ground sharply.

battement tendue A movement where the foot slides out along the ground until the toes form a point.

choreographer The person who decides what steps and movements the dancers will make and puts them all together.

corps de ballet A group of dancers who do not dance on their own or in leading roles.

en pointe When a ballet dancer stands on the tips of her toes.

grande battements Exercises that strengthen the legs and help the dancer raise their legs higher.

leotard With or without sleeves, a close-fitting costume worn for ballet classes.

mime To act out without words.

pas de deux A dance for two ballet dancers, usually male and female.

pirouette A step for which a dancer needs perfect balance and strength to spin on one leg.

plié The knees bend for this basic ballet movement.

posture Holding the head and back straight is a must for a dancer.

props Look like the "real thing" but are lighter; used by performers on stage.

solo A dance for one person.

tiara A crown often placed on a ballerina's head.

tights A skintight garment from waist to toes worn by dancers.

turn-out The way a dancer's leg turns out from the hip socket.

tutu A ballerina's skirt.